Star Signs
at Work

Star Signs at Work

Using astrology for success and harmony in the workplace

Debbie Burns

Red Wheel
Boston, MA / York Beach, ME

Contents

STAR SIGN	DATES*	SYMBOL
Aries	March 21–April 19	The Ram
Taurus	April 20–May 20	The Bull
Gemini	May 21–June 20	The Twins
Cancer	June 21–July 22	The Crab
Leo	July 23–August 22	The Lion
Virgo	August 23–September 22	The Virgin
Libra	September 23–October 22	The Scales
Scorpio	October 23–November 21	The Scorpion
Sagittarius	November 22–December 21	The Archer
Capricorn	December 22–January 19	The Goat
Aquarius	January 20–February 18	The Water Carrier
Pisces	February 19–March 20	The Fish

* The dates for each sign can differ according to what you're reading. Astrologers interpret the commencement of each season slightly differently. This affects the changeover dates for some of the signs. Your birthday may be on the "cusp" – it may fall directly on or be on either side of the dates above. If this is the case, read about both of the relevant signs to get the full picture.

For the specific associations for each sign, see the table on page 79.

Introduction

How often have you been asked, "What do you do for a living?" when you meet someone for the first time? These days, personal and social identity seem to be shaped by career choice and job titles, qualifications and salary.

How often, too, have you been asked, "What is your star sign?" Astrology is highly popular today, and it's a good starting point for discussion in both your social and your professional life.

Star Signs at Work

Your star sign represents your individual sense of identity, level of vitality and willpower, as well as your potential and your life's purpose. This book helps you explore the ways your star sign influences your professional life. Working through it will enable you to identify your natural talents and ideal career choices, and discover your potential for compatibility with other star signs in the workplace. It will also allow you to understand others at work and improve your communication with them.

Using this Book

• **Background** Read pages 8–9 for a general background to astrology and its principles.

• **Links** Pages 10–13 take you a step further by exploring the links between the different signs.

• **Star sign profiles** With this knowledge base, you can use pages 14–63 to discover the professional profile for each sign. (Note: If you want to know more about people at work but don't know their star signs, the personality descriptions in this chapter will give you clues for identifying their signs.)

• **Work relations** The second part of each star sign description highlights the type of boss you can expect for each star sign, and your compatibility with colleagues according to their star signs.

• **Putting it all together** Pages 64–69 detail the optimal team combinations using your knowledge of star signs and their compatibilities.

• **Self-enhancement** Pages 70–73 focus on enhancing your work status using your knowledge of star signs, and pages 74–77 on enhancing your physical and mental well-being.

For Quick Reference

Use the table on page 5 for basic star sign details, and the table on page 79 for the major associations linked with each sign.

Star Signs in History

The Beginnings of Astrology

Astrology is the system of beliefs that says the position of the planets, the Sun and the Moon at the time of our birth influences us. Its origins go back thousands of years to very early cultures around the world, such as the Stonehenge era in the British Isles around 3000 B.C. In these early cultures, the links between the Earth's seasons, tides and planets were first identified, and astrology was first used to plan and predict the outcomes of major political and military events. Personal horoscopes were used for royalty and other prominent figures of the day.

Signs of the Zodiac

The modern twelve-sign Zodiac emerged in Babylonia around the 5th century B.C. At this time the heavens were divided into twelve 30-degree sections along a narrow circular band known as the zodiac belt. The Sun seemed to be making its annual journey along this band, taking around 30 days to pass through each of the twelve signs. The zodiac belt was seen to contain twelve distinct and stable constellations – groupings of fixed star formations that bear the names of the astrological signs. These names have come from the myths of early civilizations and perceptions at the time of the star formations in the sky.

Star Signs Today

As religion, astronomy and scientific theory began to gain momentum in the West from around the 17th century, astrology's credibility declined. It was not until the 20th century that astrology re-emerged as people came to realize that neither science nor religion had all the answers to life's big questions.

The findings of some 20th-century researchers – such as renowned scientists and psychologists Carl Jung and Hans Eysenck – confirmed that the human psyche is influenced by astrology. This helped to re-establish astrology's credibility and lent it the popularity it still possesses today.

Star Signs and their Associations

Astrologers have identified three distinct groupings among the twelve star signs. The signs can be linked in terms of their element (character type), quality (action type), or polarity (energy type). Knowing more about these groupings will tell you more about each star sign, and its links with and differences from other signs of the zodiac.

See page 79 for a table that summarizes these groupings. Use it for quick reference. The table also lists the ruling planet (page 13) for each sign.

Elements

Early cultures divided the forces of nature into four main elements – fire, air, earth and water. Each star sign has one of the elements attributed to it. Signs with the same element are believed to share basic personality characteristics.

ELEMENT	STAR SIGNS	CHARACTERISTICS
Fire	Aries, Leo, Sagittarius	Enthusiasm, confidence, passion, energy
Air	Gemini, Libra, Aquarius	Intelligence, articulateness, objectivity, idealism
Earth	Taurus, Virgo, Capricorn	Practicality, dependability, security, realism
Water	Cancer, Scorpio, Pisces	Emotion, sensitivity, intuition, creativity

Qualities

The twelve star signs are divided into three groups of qualities. Each group represents a different point in a season, and its member signs are oriented toward action in different ways. Cardinal signs are those that appear at the beginning of a season, fixed signs those that are dominant when a season is at its peak, and mutable signs are those that appear at the end of a season.

QUALITY	STAR SIGNS	ORIENTATION TO ACTION
Cardinal	Aries, Cancer, Libra, Capricorn	Spontaneous, restless, initiating
Fixed	Taurus, Leo, Scorpio, Aquarius	Stable, enduring, committed
Mutable	Gemini, Virgo, Sagittarius, Pisces	Adaptable, flexible, cohesive

Polarities

In terms of expressing energy, the star signs can be placed in two opposing yet complementary groups: the positive and negative polarities. The polarities are believed to correspond to modern day psychology's classic extroverted–introverted personality typology. Those in the positive polarity group are spontaneous and expressive, and those in the negative polarity group are reflective and passive.

POLARITY	STAR SIGNS	ENERGY TYPE
Positive (extroverted)	Aries, Gemini, Leo, Libra, Sagittarius, Aquarius	Impulsive, excitable, communicative, social
Negative (introverted)	Taurus, Cancer, Virgo, Scorpio, Capricorn, Pisces	Receptive, sensitive, retiring, private

Ruling Planets

Each star sign is also associated with a particular planet or planets. In astrology, the celestial bodies around the Earth, including the Sun and the Moon, are called planets. Each planet has specific attributes and is said to "rule over" a sign.

Knowing which planet rules your star sign will help you identify the predominant character traits of that sign. Look out for these traits if you don't know the star sign of someone at work.

PLANET	STAR SIGN/S	ASSOCIATIONS
Sun	Leo	Individuality, creativity, spirit, willpower, vitality
Moon	Cancer	Emotion, intuition, nurturing, the past, heritage
Mercury	Gemini/Virgo	Communication, intellect, decision making
Venus	Taurus/Libra	Relationships, social values, beauty/love, harmony
Mars	Aries/Scorpio*	Energy, impulsive action, instincts
Jupiter	Sagittarius/Pisces	Growth, opportunity, good fortune, optimism,
Saturn	Capricorn/ Aquarius*	Discipline, authority, responsibility, maturity, wisdom
Uranus	Aquarius*	Individuality, freedom, independence, innovation
Neptune	Pisces	Psychic powers, escapism, mysticism, sacrifice, uncertainty
Pluto	Scorpio*	Regeneration, transformation, evolution, rebirth

*Scorpio's ruling planet is Pluto by day and Mars by night. Aquarius's ruling planet is Uranus by day and Saturn by night.

Star Signs at Work: Profiles and Compatibilities

- About the star sign
- Ideal careers/career areas
- The star sign at work
- Ideal work environment
- Personality pointers
- The boss's star sign
- Colleagues' star signs
- Compatibility tables

STAR SIGN	IDEAL CAREERS/CAREER AREAS
Aries	Professional sportsperson, corporate executive, entrepreneur, firefighter, lifesaver
Taurus	Accountant, banker, agriculturist, florist, landscape gardener, massage therapist, historian, museum/gallery manager, art collector/dealer
Gemini	Interpreter, TV presenter, journalist, sociologist, editor, writer; sales, marketing, public relations
Cancer	Interior decorator, homemaker, nurse, day-care worker, social worker, antiques dealer, chef, counselor, hotel manager
Leo	Company executive, actor, TV presenter, sales manager, charity executive, freedom fighter, fashion designer
Virgo	Accountant, bookkeeper, researcher, academic, dietician, executive assistant; finance, administration, science
Libra	Lawyer, judge, politician, diplomat, presenter, psychologist; marketing, sales, public relations
Scorpio	Secret agent, private investigator, detective, scientist, researcher, analyst, pharmacist, doctor, surgeon, security guard
Sagittarius	Travel agent, photographic journalist, park ranger, freelance "anything," travel writer/reporter, taxi driver, zoologist, union activist, sociologist
Capricorn	Manager, banker, architect, engineer, analyst, bookkeeper, dentist, IT professional, archeologist, anthropologist
Aquarius	Scientist, writer, inventor, engineer; problem solving, electronics, analysis, humanitarianism
Pisces	Artist, writer, actor, dancer, musician, nurse, counselor, priest/minister, astrologer, numerologist

Aries – The Ram

MARCH 21–APRIL 19

The Ram symbolizes the Arian's impulsive and forceful approach to life.
SIGNATURE THEME: Initiation

ASSOCIATIONS	CHARACTERISTICS
PLANET: Mars	Energy, action, impulsive desires, animal instincts
POLARITY: Positive	Impulsivity, excitability, communicativeness, sociability
ELEMENT: Fire	Enthusiasm, confidence, passion, energy
QUALITY: Cardinal	Spontaneity, restlessness, desire for action

ARIES is the first sign of the zodiac and represents eternal youth. No matter their age, Arians have bottomless pits of energy, and loads of enthusiasm and curiosity. They propel themselves headfirst into the world each day with no fear or reservations. With their sights planted clearly ahead, Arians have little respect for tradition or convention. This can sometimes create friction. Passionate, fearless and impulsive, Arians are often attracted to reckless activities and hair-raising adventures.

Arians at Work

At work Arians are highly competitive and driven, big-picture people who can quickly create action plans and initiate projects. Goal oriented and reward focused, Arians are easily motivated to excel. They make forceful change agents.

Ideal Work Environment

Arians need constant challenge and frequent change in their work environments if they are to stay stimulated. They are at their best in difficult situations that require quick decision making and action. Whatever their endeavors, however, Arians need space to move and the ability to set their own agenda and pace.

IDEAL CAREERS/CAREER AREAS
Professional sportsperson, corporate executive, entrepreneur, firefighter, lifesaver

Personality Pointers

Arians can be dynamic, impulsive, assertive, resilient, impatient, driven, independent, direct, and reckless. Personal development areas: learning compromise, empathy and judgment.

The Aries Boss

Arians make demanding and motivating leaders. Their competitive streak means they will rarely recognize or accept defeat, and they are prone to setting unrealistic expectations for themselves and others. On the up side, the Aries boss leads by example and is openly appreciative of others' initiative and hard work. You will always know where you stand with the very direct and frank Aries boss.

Work Compatibility

Aries:

• Is most compatible with other extroverted signs associated with fire and air: Leo, Sagittarius, Gemini, Aquarius.
• Faces possible conflict with signs sharing the same quality – cardinal signs and/or those associated with water: Cancer, Libra, Capricorn, Scorpio, Pisces.
• May form a surprisingly useful pairing with the remaining signs associated with earth: Taurus, Virgo.

ARIES PARTNERSHIPS

ARIES WITH	COMMENT
Aries	Exhausting – too much competition and impulsiveness to be beneficial.
Taurus	Productive – much will be accomplished together.
Gemini	Stimulating – innovation will flourish.
Cancer	Frustrating – respect for each other's values and approach to life will be lacking.
Leo	Dynamic – a powerhouse of creativity and energy.
Virgo	Supportive – Aries will be happy at the helm and Virgo will be contented behind the scenes.
Libra	Stubborn – both signs will hold tightly to their own ideals and perspectives.
Scorpio	Alienating – each sign will work to undermine the other's success.
Sagittarius	Adventurous – opportunities will be seized and outcomes will be rewarding.
Capricorn	Challenging – there will be a lack of agreement and envy of each other's gains.
Aquarius	Different – eccentricity and novelty will flourish.
Pisces	Insensitive – mutual understanding and rapport will be lacking.

Taurus – The Bull

APRIL 20–MAY 20

The Bull is a symbol of Taurus's strong instincts and persevering nature.

SIGNATURE THEME: Stability

ASSOCIATIONS	CHARACTERISTICS
PLANET: Venus	Relationships, social values, beauty/love, harmony
POLARITY: Negative	Receptivity, sensitivity, reserve, desire for privacy
ELEMENT: Earth	Practicality, dependability, security, realism
QUALITY: Fixed	Stability, loyalty, endurance

TAURUS is a practical, down-to-earth sign concerned with creature comforts and long-term security. Taureans have a methodical, well-planned approach to life, preferring to leave little to chance. If they believe something is worth having, they can be quite determined and focused until successful. Taurus is one of the most patient and determined signs.

Taureans at Work

Productive and focused, Taureans are at their best when using their hands and providing the "muscle" behind projects to ensure their success. Taureans work hard to maintain the status quo in their chosen profession, often resisting change – particularly if it has been thrust upon them. They value organizational rules and principles, and religiously follow stated policies and procedures.

Ideal Work Environment

Financial security is a high priority, so well-established and stable businesses that offer tenure and steady advancement attract Taureans. Quiet and aesthetically pleasing surroundings are also important. Taureans prefer operating alone or behind the scenes. Museums, galleries and anything involving flora and fauna will also suit them.

 IDEAL CAREERS/CAREER AREAS
Accountant, banker, agriculturist, florist, landscape gardener, massage therapist, historian, museum/gallery manager, art collector/dealer

Personality Pointers

Taureans can be stable, steadfast, patient, resourceful, stubborn, dedicated, sensual, and self-indulgent. Personal development areas: learning to embrace change and innovation, and to be adaptable and flexible.

The Taurus Boss

Taureans make for reluctant leaders as they shy away from the limelight. However, they will be conservative, calm and methodical if they find themselves in leadership positions. Taureans prefer dealing with the facts, and will take their time gathering and analyzing information before forming opinions and making decisions. They value hard work and commitment in others and in return are fair and patient people managers.

Work Compatibility

Taurus:

• Is most compatible with other introverted signs associated with earth and water: Virgo, Capricorn, Cancer, Pisces.

• Faces possible conflict with signs sharing the same quality – fixed signs and/or those associated with air: Leo, Scorpio, Aquarius, Gemini, Libra.

• May form a surprisingly useful pairing with the remaining signs associated with fire: Aries, Sagittarius.

TAURUS PARTNERSHIPS

TAURUS WITH	COMMENT
Aries	Productive – much will be accomplished together.
Taurus	Successful – it will be all work and no play when two Taureans get together.
Gemini	Annoying – Gemini will want to talk while Taurus will want to work.
Cancer	Receptive – both signs will feel appreciated and supported.
Leo	Controlling – strong wills and personality styles will conflict.
Virgo	Scrupulous – everything will be doubled checked, and nothing overlooked.
Libra	Lazy – both signs have a tendency toward self-indulgence.
Scorpio	Stubborn – each will refuse to give way to the other's suggestions.
Sagittarius	Active – no stop signs will be needed when these two get together.
Capricorn	Harmonious – Capricorn will be happily in charge and Taurus contented behind the scenes.
Aquarius	Alienating – neither sign will understand or appreciate the other.
Pisces	Intuitive – the signs will unite to hone their perception and intuition.

Gemini – The Twins

MAY 21–JUNE 20

The Twins signify Gemini's dual nature and drive to connect with others.

SIGNATURE THEME: Communication

ASSOCIATIONS	CHARACTERISTICS
PLANET: Mercury	Communication, intellectual ability, decision making
POLARITY: Positive	Impulsivity, excitability, communicativeness, sociability
ELEMENT: Air	Intelligence, articulateness, objectivity, idealism
QUALITY: Mutable	Adaptability, flexibility, cohesiveness

GEMINIS are the gifted communicators of the zodiac. Their quest is for connection with others, achieved through mutual understanding. Blessed with natural talents, they are able to communicate effectively with others on many different wavelengths and subjects. With such versatile and active minds, Geminis can border on genius one day and can be lost the next day in a sea of contrast and paradox – hence the duality of the star-sign symbol.

Gemini at Work

Geminis usually find success easily in their professional lives. They have the "gift of the gab" and innate interpersonal and presentation skills; this assures them of much support and fanfare. Their addiction to reading and self-education means they naturally embody the concept of lifelong learning, and they will be employable up to and well beyond retirement.

Ideal Work Environment

Gemini needs a constantly changing, even pressurized, work environment to sustain their interest and keep them mentally stimulated. They need to work with people who can keep them on track and provide instant feedback on their ideas. Left alone or unchallenged, Geminis can become rudderless and unproductive.

IDEAL CAREERS/CAREER AREAS

Interpreter, TV presenter, journalist, sociologist, editor, writer, sales, marketing, public relations

Personality Pointers

Geminis can be persuasive, eloquent, curious, inquisitive, superficial, witty, charming, and flippant. Personal development areas: developing initiative, tenacity and focus.

The Gemini Boss

Gemini bosses are approachable and popular. They prize open communication in the office and make skilled managers of difficult people. Encouraging and motivating to all, they use their social skills to lower political barriers and build productive teams. It is essential to give them plenty of administrative support, delegating their more mundane tasks.

Work Compatibility

Gemini:

• Is most compatible with other extroverted signs associated with air and fire: Libra, Aquarius, Aries, Leo.

• Faces possible conflict with signs sharing the same quality – mutable signs and/or those associated with earth: Virgo, Sagittarius, Pisces, Capricorn, Taurus.

• May form a surprisingly useful pairing with the remaining signs associated with water: Cancer, Scorpio.

GEMINI PARTNERSHIPS

GEMINI WITH	COMMENT
Aries	Stimulating – innovation will flourish.
Taurus	Annoying – Gemini will want to talk while Taurus will want to work.
Gemini	Rudderless – there will be too many ideas and none will come to fruition.
Cancer	Creative – ideas will be supported and implemented.
Leo	Versatile – Leo will be a stable and determined associate for Gemini.
Virgo	Unsupportive – Virgo will end up doing more than the fair share of the work.
Libra	Brilliant – the mix will be politically awesome and socially dynamic.
Scorpio	Successful – the two will unite to achieve goals.
Sagittarius	Flighty – perseverance will be lacking.
Capricorn	Alienating – neither sign will understand or appreciate the other.
Aquarius	Inventive – together they will be problem-solving dynamos.
Pisces	Indecisive – mutual agreement and drive will be lacking.

Cancer – The Crab

JUNE 21–JULY 22

The Crab symbolizes Cancer's hard, protective exterior and vulnerable emotions.

SIGNATURE THEMES: Nurturing and protecting

ASSOCIATIONS	CHARACTERISTICS
PLANET: Moon	Emotions, intuition, nurturing, the past, heritage
POLARITY: Negative	Receptivity, sensitivity, reserve, desire for privacy
ELEMENT: Water	Emotion, sensitivity, intuitiveness, creativity
QUALITY: Cardinal	Spontaneity, restlessness, orientation to action

CANCER is the sign of the family and nurturing. With an instinctive need to care and to form close emotional ties, Cancerians are skilled at making an extended home and extended family of their workplace and colleagues. Their acute intuition and perception make them adept at reading others' moods and thoughts. They tend to put on a tough, bravado-filled, "no one can hurt me" exterior to shield their supersensitivity and their vulnerability to life's harsh realities.

Cancer at Work

As family is the Cancerian's priority, personal life tends to eclipse professional endeavors. Cancerians are attracted to careers that allow them to make one-on-one contact and utilize their talent for making others feel safe and comfortable. Emotional satisfaction and security are their professional goals.

Ideal Work Environment

A harmonious and close-knit work environment is essential for Cancerians' well-being. They work best in a small business or a home environment. Insecurity plagues them at the best of times and requires active management, particularly during times of change.

IDEAL CAREERS/CAREER AREAS

Interior decorator, homemaker, nurse, day-care worker, social worker, antiques dealer, chef, counselor, hotel manager

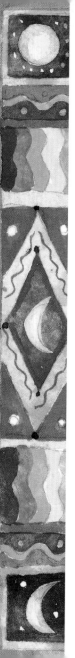

Personality Pointers

Cancerians can be protective, sentimental, sensitive, kind, compassionate, intuitive, patient, cautious, and fearful. Personal development areas: increasing objectivity, independence and confidence.

The Cancer Boss

Cancerians make kind and gentle leaders who expect efficiency and discipline from their staff. They like to create a comfortable and congenial environment where people can work and play together. Soft furnishings, family portraits and stress balls feature in their work domain. Cancer bosses value and reward cooperation and teamwork.

Work Compatibility

Cancer:

• Is most compatible with other introverted signs associated with water and earth: Scorpio, Pisces, Taurus, Virgo.

• Faces possible conflict with signs sharing the same quality – cardinal signs and/or those associated with fire: Aries, Libra, Capricorn, Leo, Sagittarius.

• May form a surprisingly useful pairing with the remaining signs associated with air: Gemini, Aquarius.

CANCER PARTNERSHIPS

CANCER WITH	COMMENT
Aries	Frustrating – respect for each other's values and approach to life will be lacking.
Taurus	Receptive – both signs will feel appreciated and supported.
Gemini	Creative – ideas will be supported and implemented.
Cancer	Supersensitive – each will take offence too readily.
Leo	Unstable – Leo bravado will intensify Cancer's insecurity.
Virgo	Respectful – each will appreciate the other's quiet and efficient manner.
Libra	Critical – each sign will only see faults in the other.
Scorpio	Productive – the two will form a great partnership.
Sagittarius	Disrespectful – the two will have opposing values and principles.
Capricorn	Annoying – Capricorn will want to scale heights and Cancer will fear them.
Aquarius	Constructive – Aquarian objectivity will be mixed with Cancerian compassion.
Pisces	Flexible – each will be willing to go out of their way for the other.

Leo – The Lion

JULY 23–AUGUST 22

The Lion symbolizes Leo's power, passion and authority.
SIGNATURE THEME: Vitalization

ASSOCIATIONS	CHARACTERISTICS
PLANET: Sun	Independence, creative drive, spirit, willpower, vitality
POLARITY: Positive	Impulsivity, excitability, communicativeness, sociability
ELEMENT: Fire	Enthusiasm, confidence, passion, energy
QUALITY: Fixed	Stability, loyalty, endurance

LEO is the charismatic and eternally optimistic sign of the zodiac. Leos' sunny-natured, vital, larger-than-life personalities ensure their popularity. They are proud and dignified, and the respect and admiration of others drive their heroic deeds and nurture their self-esteem. To play out the drama of their lives, Leos need a large stage and a willing audience.

Leo at Work

Naturally confident and charming, Leos go out of their way to achieve recognition and distinction in their chosen professions. They are competitive, testing their strength and endurance against that of others. Leos will often take up causes and lead charities, playing the hero and devising grand plans for a brighter future.

Ideal Work Environment

Leos are at home in the global arena. They rise to their rightful leadership position in times of crisis or pressure. They forge ahead courageously, heedless of obstacles. Challenging positions that thrust them upfront and into the limelight are ideal. They need interaction with others, and plenty of action and control in their daily activities.

IDEAL CAREERS/CAREER AREAS
Company executive, actor, TV presenter, sales manager, charity executive, freedom fighter, fashion designer

Personality Pointers

Leos can be proud, generous, passionate, creative, loyal, determined, courageous, arrogant, and lazy. Personal development areas: learning humility and to seek and take informed advice and ask for help when necessary.

The Leo Boss

Leo is the natural leader of the zodiac. Leos have great faith in their ability to inspire and manage others. For the Leo boss, mutual respect is important. Staff who show loyalty and commitment will be rewarded with noble deeds and generosity. Leo bosses do have to watch their zealousness and fiery strength, however, as these traits may overwhelm the quieter types and come across as arrogance.

Work Compatibility

Leo:

• Is most compatible with other extroverted signs associated with fire and air: Aries, Sagittarius, Gemini, Libra.

• Faces possible conflict with signs sharing the same quality – fixed signs and/or those associated with water: Cancer, Scorpio, Pisces, Taurus, Aquarius.

• May form a surprisingly useful pairing with the remaining signs associated with earth: Virgo, Capricorn.

LEO PARTNERSHIPS

LEO WITH	COMMENT
Aries	Dynamic – a powerhouse of creativity and energy.
Taurus	Controlling – strong wills and personal styles will conflict.
Gemini	Versatile – Leo will be a stable and determined associate for Gemini.
Cancer	Unstable – Leo bravado will intensify Cancer's insecurity.
Leo	Confusing – the question will be: who's in charge?
Virgo	Integrating – Virgo will cover the details and Leo will take the lead.
Libra	Successful – Leo's charisma will blend with Libra's political savvy.
Scorpio	Suspicious – each sign will misread the other's intent.
Sagittarius	Productive – these signs will make a great partnership.
Capricorn	Competitive – these signs will share a healthy competitive spirit.
Aquarius	Inconsistent – Leo will live for today, Aquarius for tomorrow.
Pisces	One-way – Leo will intimidate and Pisces will cower.

Virgo – The Virgin
AUGUST 23–SEPTEMBER 22

The Virgin symbolizes Virgo's drive for perfection and veiled sensuality.
SIGNATURE THEME: Analysis

ASSOCIATIONS	CHARACTERISTICS
PLANET: Mercury	Communication, intellectual ability, decision making
POLARITY: Negative	Receptivity, sensitivity, reserve, desire for privacy
ELEMENT: Earth	Practicality, dependability, security, realism
QUALITY: Mutable	Adaptability, flexibility, cohesiveness

VIRGO is the most cool, calm and collected sign of the zodiac. Sensible and meticulous, Virgoans win the respect of the other, less-focused signs. Practical and analytical, able to categorize large amounts of information, they have razor-sharp perception and probing minds. They bring improved efficiency and effectiveness, but their drive for perfectionism can breed narrow-mindedness and fussiness.

Virgo at Work

At work Virgoans come across as efficient, methodical, astute and logical. They put their heads down and bury themselves in the details of their tasks, with little awareness of the interpersonal aspects of office life. They set very high standards for themselves. This can be stressful – unless they receive regular feedback on their efforts and performance.

Ideal Work Environment

Virgoans prefer order and structure. An office environment, library or science laboratory is the ideal workplace. They need to feel useful and are happiest when providing support to others or using their sharp intellects to identify and fix problems. Virgoans do not operate well in isolation or in a constantly changing environment.

IDEAL CAREERS/CAREER AREAS
Accountant, bookkeeper, researcher, academic, dietician, executive assistant; finance, administration, science

Personality Pointers

Virgoans can be practical, adaptable, discerning, organized, reliable, critical, efficient, logical, and fussy. Personal development areas: accepting that "to err is human," setting realistic expectations, and learning to say "No."

The Virgo Boss

Virgoans' talents do not lend themselves naturally to the leadership role – unless it's the operations or finance side of a business that's being managed. Virgo bosses can be openly critical and sticklers for rules and regulations. They expect punctuality, attention to detail and efficiency from their staff. In return, they are good at clarifying responsibilities, providing clear direction and prioritizing work effectively.

Work Compatibility

Virgo:

• Is most compatible with other introverted signs associated with earth and water: Taurus, Capricorn, Cancer, Scorpio.

• Faces possible conflict with signs sharing the same quality – mutable signs and/or those associated with air: Gemini, Sagittarius, Pisces, Aquarius, Libra.

• May form a surprisingly useful pairing with the remaining signs associated with fire: Aries, Leo.

VIRGO PARTNERSHIPS

VIRGO WITH	COMMENT
Aries	Supportive – Aries will be happy at the helm and Virgo contented behind the scenes.
Taurus	Scrupulous – everything will be doubled checked, and nothing will be overlooked.
Gemini	Unsupportive – Virgo will end up doing more than the fair share of the work.
Cancer	Respectful – each will appreciate the other's quiet and efficient manner.
Leo	Integrating – Virgo will cover the details and Leo will take the lead.
Virgo	Puritanical – expectations will be unrealistic and mistakes unforgiven.
Libra	One-sided – Libra will take advantage of Virgo's dedication to task.
Scorpio	Determined – both signs will work diligently and cooperatively.
Sagittarius	Frustrating – structured Virgo won't be able to work with spontaneous Sagittarius.
Capricorn	Capable – the signs will complement each other and productivity will be high.
Aquarius	Conflicting – Virgo's set ways will conflict with Aquarian ideals.
Pisces	Uncomfortable – Pisces' wavering emotions will cause stable Virgo discomfort.

Libra – The Scales

SEPTEMBER 23–OCTOBER 22

The Scales symbolize Libra's challenge to find a balance between personal desires and the needs of others.

SIGNATURE THEME: Balance

ASSOCIATIONS	CHARACTERISTICS
PLANET: Venus	Relationships, social values, beauty/love, harmony
POLARITY: Positive	Impulsivity, excitability, communicativeness, sociability
ELEMENT: Air	Intelligence, articulateness, objectivity, idealism
QUALITY: Cardinal	Spontaneous, restless, action oriented

LIBRA is the sign of justice and represents fair play and partnership. Full of diplomacy and tact, Librans like to contribute to discussions and debates in order to encourage differing factions to unite, help others find common ground and right the wronged. Idealistically driven to find a way to please everyone, they can at times appear insincere. They may struggle inwardly when their own desires conflict with the expectations and approval of others.

Libra at Work

Librans, more than other star signs, need to have people around them. They can be found anywhere other than at their desks, preferring to congregate in hallways, tearooms and open work spaces in order to discuss the latest in office happenings. Librans are the supreme networkers of the zodiac.

Ideal Work Environment

Librans' ideal environment must be relaxing and harmonious. However, it is not so much the physical environment that counts as the need to feel accepted and valued by those with whom they work. Hence, for Librans to be happy at work, the culture of the work environment must encourage open communication and the sharing of ideas.

IDEAL CAREERS/CAREER AREAS
Lawyer, judge, politician, diplomat, presenter, psychologist; marketing, sales, public relations

Personality Pointers

Librans can be diplomatic, thoughtful, intelligent, vain, charming, sophisticated, sociable, and indecisive. Personal development areas: addressing procrastination, accepting confrontation when required and confronting others if needed, and lessening dependence on the approval of others.

The Libra Boss

Libran bosses have a people-focused and inclusive management style. They will take the time to get to know and relate to each of their staff members. They will encourage the input and ideas of each individual, no matter how unrealistic. Libran bosses will use their charm to obtain agreement, and are adept at resolving disputes. They can at times become opinionated if their gentle manipulations do not produce the desired effect.

Work Compatibility

Libra:

• Is most compatible with other extroverted signs associated with air and fire: Gemini, Aquarius, Leo, Sagittarius.

• Faces possible conflict with signs sharing the same quality – cardinal signs and/or those associated with earth: Aries, Cancer, Capricorn, Taurus, Virgo.

• May form a surprisingly useful pairing with the remaining signs associated with water: Scorpio, Pisces.

LIBRA PARTNERSHIPS

LIBRA WITH	COMMENT
Aries	Stubborn – both signs will hold tightly to their own ideals and perspectives.
Taurus	Lazy – both signs have a tendency toward self-indulgence.
Gemini	Brilliant – the mix will be politically awesome and socially dynamic.
Cancer	Critical – each sign will only see faults in the other.
Leo	Successful – Leo's charisma will blend with Libra's political savvy.
Virgo	One-sided – Libra will take advantage of Virgo's dedication to task.
Libra	Pleasant – mutual consideration and inclusiveness will reign.
Scorpio	Respectful – each will admire the other's pursuit of truth and understanding.
Sagittarius	Agreeable – these signs will soon strike a workable deal between themselves.
Capricorn	Insincere – Capricorn directness will provoke Libra into confrontation.
Aquarius	Creative – ideas will flourish.
Pisces	Harmonious – each will give the other a great deal of consideration.

Scorpio – The Scorpion
23 OCTOBER–21 NOVEMBER

The Scorpion symbolizes Scorpio's deep and mysterious emotions and strong instincts.

SIGNATURE THEME: Transformation

ASSOCIATIONS	CHARACTERISTICS
PLANETS: Pluto	Regeneration, transformation, evolution, rebirth
Mars	Energy, action, impulsive desires, animal instincts
POLARITY: Negative	Receptivity, sensitivity, reserve, desire for privacy
ELEMENT: Water	Emotion, sensitivity, intuitiveness, creativity
QUALITY: Fixed	Stability, loyalty, endurance

SCORPIO is the intensely mysterious, impenetrable sign of the zodiac. Driven by their secret desires and a need for emotional fulfillment, Scorpios can shift from being passionate and sensual one minute to being icy cold and indifferent the next. Scorpios take a focused and totally committed approach to everything. Their mental radar and highly developed probing skills ensure that little misses their attention and critical assessment.

Scorpio at Work

Scorpios harbor a desire to succeed, and can patiently work away in the background to satisfy their long-held ambitions. They are passionate about precision, and have a knack for problem solving and focused attention in the most challenging of situations.

Ideal Work Environment

A secure and functional environment is the ideal of Scorpios. Hospitals and scientific and medical laboratories attract them. Their offices hold textbooks and journals and the latest in technological equipment. They prefer to work independently rather than in a team, but are skilled at shutting out distractions if working with others nearby is necessary.

IDEAL CAREERS/CAREER AREAS
Secret agent, private investigator, detective, scientist, researcher, analyst, pharmacist, doctor, surgeon, security guard

Personality Pointers

Scorpios can be sensual, imaginative, jealous, protective, intense, penetrating, secretive, and manipulative. Personal development areas: easing up on self-criticism and sharing more of the self with others.

The Scorpio Boss

Scorpio bosses are spirited and intuitive. They demand competence and loyalty from their staff and will quickly discard those who don't meet the mark. Scorpios are extremely skilled at general management positions involving all areas of business. Scorpio bosses in these roles will be able to use their talent for organizational strategy and transformation.

Work Compatibility

Scorpio:

• Is most compatible with other introverted signs associated with water and earth: Cancer, Pisces, Virgo, Capricorn.

• Faces possible conflict with signs sharing the same quality – fixed signs and/or those associated with fire: Taurus, Leo, Aquarius, Aries, Sagittarius.

• May form a surprisingly useful pairing with the remaining signs associated with air: Libra, Gemini.

♏♏♏♏♏♏♏♏♏

SCORPIO PARTNERSHIPS

SCORPIO WITH	COMMENT
Aries	Alienating – each sign will work to undermine the other's success.
Taurus	Stubborn – each will refuse to give way to the other's suggestions.
Gemini	Successful – the two will unite to achieve goals.
Cancer	Productive – the two will form a great partnership.
Leo	Suspicious – each sign will misread the other's intent.
Virgo	Determined – both signs will work diligently and cooperatively.
Libra	Respectful – each will admire the other's pursuit of truth and understanding.
Scorpio	Innovative – two Scorpios together could make pioneering advances.
Sagittarius	Frustrating – Sagittarius' fiery impatience will irritate focused Scorpio.
Capricorn	Productive – each will encourage the ambitions of the other.
Aquarius	Conflicting – Scorpio's nature will conflict with Aquarian ideals.
Pisces	Supportive – working together, both signs will find emotional harmony.

Sagittarius – The Archer

22 NOVEMBER–21 DECEMBER

The Archer symbolizes Sagittarius' dual nature of half-man and half-beast.

SIGNATURE THEME: Exploration

ASSOCIATIONS	CHARACTERISTICS
PLANET: Jupiter	Expansion, opportunity, good fortune, luck, optimism, wealth
POLARITY: Positive	Impulsivity, excitability, communicativeness, sociability
ELEMENT: Fire	Enthusiasm, confidence, passion, energy
QUALITY: Mutable	Adaptability, flexibility, cohesiveness

SAGITTARIUS is the adventurous, freedom-loving sign of the zodiac. Sagittarians constantly need movement, excitement and change. This can create a general restlessness and reluctance to commit to long-range plans. Sagittarians are happy-go-lucky and fun loving. They take risks and enjoy danger, which means they can sometimes live to regret their decisions and actions.

Sagittarius at Work

Sagittarians make optimistic and enthusiastic work colleagues. Any occupation that provides freedom of thought and/or travel will suit them. Their restlessness can result in frequent job changes, and many won't find their niche till later in life. Sagittarians' disdain for convention often works against any ambition they may have to climb the corporate ladder.

Ideal Work Environment

Sagittarians work best in open environments with as few rules and restrictions as possible. They need constant challenges and change in order to focus their energy and quench their thirst for variety. Any outdoor environment will suit, and the advent of the "virtual" office, which allows people to work from anywhere, is exciting to them.

 ## IDEAL CAREERS/CAREER AREAS

Travel agent, photographic journalist, park ranger, freelance "anything," travel writer/reporter, taxi driver, zoologist, union activist, sociologist

Personality Pointers

Sagittarians can be adventurous, bold, optimistic, honest, impulsive, energetic, impatient, frank, open-minded, and independent. Personal development areas: working on tactfulness, timing and objective analysis.

The Sagittarius Boss

Sagittarians make for eager and optimistic leaders. They like to be kept busy with many different projects at once, and will ensure their staff are doing the same. They have a knack for boosting office morale, sharing their opinions and delegating the more mundane tasks. The Sagittarian boss will frequently be absent from the office, taking up every opportunity for overseas or interstate travel.

Work Compatibility

Sagittarius:

• Is most compatible with other extroverted signs associated with fire and air: Aries, Leo, Libra, Aquarius.

• Faces possible conflict with signs sharing the same quality – mutable signs and/or those associated with water: Gemini, Virgo, Pisces, Cancer, Scorpio.

• May form a surprisingly useful pairing with the remaining signs associated with earth: Taurus, Capricorn.

SAGITTARIUS PARTNERSHIPS

SAGITTARIUS WITH	COMMENT
Aries	Adventurous – opportunities will be seized and outcomes will be rewarding.
Taurus	Active – no stop signs will be needed when these two get together.
Gemini	Flighty – perseverance will be lacking.
Cancer	Disrespectful – the two will have opposing values and principles.
Leo	Productive – these signs will make a great partnership.
Virgo	Frustrating – structured Virgo won't be able to work with spontaneous Sagittarius.
Libra	Agreeable – these signs will soon strike a workable deal between themselves.
Scorpio	Frustrating – Sagittarius' fiery impatience will irritate focused Scorpio.
Sagittarius	Lucky – double doses of optimism and risk taking will result in large doses of luck.
Capricorn	Maturing – Capricorn will provide Sagittarius with structure and maturity.
Aquarius	Versatile – Aquarian ideas will be fueled by Sagittarian energy.
Pisces	Unstable – neither sign will help the other to find and appreciate stability.

Capricorn – The Goat
DECEMBER 22–JANUARY 19

The goat symbolizes Capricorn's ambitious and industrious nature.

SIGNATURE THEME: Achievement

ASSOCIATIONS	CHARACTERISTICS
PLANET: Saturn	Discipline, authority, responsibility, maturity, wisdom
POLARITY: Negative	Receptivity, sensitivity, reserve, desire for privacy
ELEMENT: Earth	Practicality, dependability, security, realism
QUALITY: Cardinal	Spontaneity, restlessness, orientation to action

CAPRICORN is the most ambitious and disciplined of the signs. Capricorns take life seriously, and have a cautious and steady approach. Respectful and dependable, they have a strong sense of duty and are concerned about financial security. Their black-and-white approach to life can sometimes make them dictatorial and moralistic.

Capricorn at Work

Capricorns are ambitious and driven. From an early age, they set their sights high on the corporate ladder. They are attracted to power, status and financial reward and will work hard to achieve these. They take their responsibilities seriously and readily accept accountability for their actions. They usually like to work alone and at a steady pace. They have a knack for turning conceptual ideas into practical reality.

Ideal Work Environment

Capricorns like a structured, traditional work environment where their responsibilities are clearly outlined. Organizations that offer tenure and career progression suit them. Capricorns' resistance to change and their attraction to convention make a stable, predictable environment ideal for them.

 ### IDEAL CAREERS/CAREER AREAS
Manager, banker, architect, engineer, analyst, bookkeeper, dentist, IT professional, archeologist, anthropologist

Personality Pointers

Capricorns can be ambitious, disciplined, materialistic, conventional, practical, cautious, scrupulous, organized, trustworthy, and resourceful. Personal development areas: learning to lighten up, to relax and take time out, to trust in others' abilities, and to play office "politics."

The Capricorn Boss

Capricorn bosses feel quite at home in any management position. They make considerate leaders who expect and reward obedience, dedication and competence. Capricorn bosses practice what they preach and are consummate professionals. They like control and are passionate devotees to the Total Quality Management concept.

Work Compatibility

Capricorn:

• Is most compatible with other introverted signs associated with earth and water: Taurus, Virgo, Scorpio, Pisces.

• Faces possible conflict with signs sharing the same quality – cardinal signs and/or those associated with air: Aries, Cancer, Libra, Gemini, Aquarius.

• May form a surprisingly useful pairing with the remaining signs associated with fire: Leo, Sagittarius.

CAPRICORN PARTNERSHIPS

CAPRICORN WITH	COMMENT
Aries	Challenging – there will be lack of agreement and envy of each other's gains.
Taurus	Harmonious – Capricorn will be happily in charge and Taurus will be contented behind the scenes.
Gemini	Alienating – neither will understand or appreciate the other.
Cancer	Annoying – Capricorn will want to scale heights and Cancer will fear them.
Leo	Competitive – these signs will share a healthy competitive spirit.
Virgo	Capable – the signs will complement each other and productivity will be high.
Libra	Insincere – Capricorn directness will provoke Libra into confrontation.
Scorpio	Productive – each will encourage the ambitions of the other.
Sagittarius	Maturing – Capricorn will provide Sagittarius with structure and maturity.
Capricorn	Successful – each will encourage the ambitions of the other.
Aquarius	Disrespectful – the two will hold opposing values and principles.
Pisces	Adaptable – Pisces will provide flexibility and Capricorn direction.

Aquarius – The Water Carrier

JANUARY 20–FEBRUARY 18

The Water Carrier symbolizes the volume of intuitive knowledge that Aquarius holds.

SIGNATURE THEME: Illumination

ASSOCIATIONS	CHARACTERISTICS
PLANETS: Uranus	Individuality, freedom, independence, innovation
Saturn	Discipline, authority, responsibility, maturity, wisdom
POLARITY: Positive	Impulsivity, excitability, communicativeness, sociability
ELEMENT: Air	Intelligence, articulateness, objectivity, idealism
QUALITY: Fixed	Stability, loyalty, endurance

AQUARIUS is the most eccentric sign. Aquarians have a powerful intellect and an independent, fertile imagination. Gifted at thinking on their feet, they demonstrate their intuitive powers when dealing with others. They mostly appear calm and relaxed, but can be absentminded. They have their own notion of time and find it difficult to conform to rules and set procedures. Aquarians' vision and humanitarianism often see them deeply concerned about the plight of others.

Aquarius at Work

At work Aquarians are often perceived as aloof and a bit eccentric, as they can become preoccupied with the ideas racing through their heads. They need an occupation that challenges their intellect, and sufficient freedom and time to devise innovative plans. Until they find their niche Aquarians can be restless and unsettled, and this can create open conflict and antagonism toward management.

Ideal Work Environment

Aquarians need an emotionally stable and noise-free environment, free of complex regulations and politics, in order to feel comfortable and to release their innovative powers. They avoid routine tasks and physically demanding jobs.

 IDEAL CAREERS/CAREER AREAS
Scientist, writer, inventor, engineer; problem solving, electronics, analysis, humanitarianism

Personality Pointers

Aquarians can be intelligent, independent, idealistic, inventive, charitable, eccentric, voyeuristic, communicative, neurotic, and full of vision. Personal development areas: working on emotional involvement, productivity and the ability to perform within constraints.

The Aquarius Boss

Aquarians are not generally attracted to leadership positions. They lack respect for the many policies and procedures inherent in the role, and hope the people issues will sort themselves out without the need for their intervention. Their contribution is their forward-thinking and relaxed approach. Those falling under their responsibility will be highly stimulated, encouraged to contribute ideas and solutions, and provided with the necessary freedom and technology to make this happen.

Work Compatibility

Aquarius:

• Is most compatible with other extroverted signs associated with air and fire: Gemini, Libra, Aries, Sagittarius.

• Faces possible conflict with signs sharing the same quality – fixed signs and/or those associated with earth: Leo, Scorpio, Taurus, Virgo, Capricorn.

• May form a surprisingly useful pairing with the remaining signs associated with water: Cancer, Pisces.

AQUARIUS PARTNERSHIPS

AQUARIUS WITH	COMMENT
Aries	Different – eccentricity and novelty will flourish.
Taurus	Alienating – neither sign will understand or appreciate the other.
Gemini	Inventive – together they will be problem-solving dynamos.
Cancer	Constructive – Aquarian objectivity will be mixed with Cancerian compassion.
Leo	Inconsistent – Leo will live for today, Aquarius for tomorrow.
Virgo	Conflicting – Virgo's set ways will conflict with Aquarian ideals.
Libra	Creative – ideas will flourish.
Scorpio	Conflicting – Scorpio's nature will conflict with Aquarian ideals.
Sagittarius	Versatile – Aquarian ideas will be fueled by Sagittarian energy.
Capricorn	Disrespectful – the two will hold opposing values and principles.
Aquarius	High-impact – together the two will be capable of changing global consciousness.
Pisces	Complementary – Pisces will provide Aquarius with emotional awareness.

Pisces – The Fish
FEBRUARY 19–MARCH 20

The fish swimming in opposite directions symbolize Pisceans' need to balance their inner emotions with their external reality.

SIGNATURE THEME: Sensitivity

ASSOCIATIONS	CHARACTERISTICS
PLANETS: Neptune	Psychic powers, escapism, mysticism, sacrifice, uncertainty
Jupiter	Expansion, opportunity, good fortune, luck, optimism, wealth
POLARITY: Negative	Receptivity, sensitivity, reserve, desire for privacy
ELEMENT: Water	Emotion, sensitivity, intuitiveness, creativity
QUALITY: Mutable	Adaptability, flexibility, cohesiveness

PISCES is a sign concerned with the emotions, creativity and the psychic world. Imagination and spirituality come naturally to the dreamy Pisceans. They have quiet, peaceful, romantic natures, as well as exceptional intuition and an active sixth sense. They are emotional sponges and may sometimes live in an inner world of turbulent feelings. They value their accurate perception of others' feelings and moods, and adjust easily to changing emotional currents.

Pisces at Work

Pisceans are versatile, adaptable and quick to acclimatize to the organizational culture. Their ability to listen, empathize and build rapport ensures they are well liked and accepted throughout the organization. They find it easy to make friends with their colleagues and enjoy the social aspects of working with others.

Ideal Work Environment

Pisceans require a fluid, non-restrictive environment in order to free their self-expression. Aesthetically pleasing surroundings such as museums, galleries and theaters are ideal for them. They value the opportunity to self-direct their daily tasks and priorities. Their profound personal integrity and social consciousness are fully utilized when they are helping others one-on-one.

IDEAL CAREERS/CAREER AREAS
Artist, writer, actor, dancer, musician, nurse, counselor, priest/minister, astrologer, numerologist

Personality Pointers

Pisceans can be intuitive, sensitive, imaginative, romantic, creative, kind, compassionate, flexible, emotional, trusting, expressive, gentle, and gullible. Personal development areas: establishing personal boundaries, setting goals and sticking with them until achieved, and increasing initiative.

The Pisces Boss

We rarely find Pisceans in leadership roles – management is not something Pisceans usually aspire to. However, they do make gentle and compassionate managers who value freedom of speech among their staff and contributions from individuals. Piscean bosses are skilled at building cohesive teams that appreciate the space and consideration given to them.

Work Compatibility

Pisces:

• Is most compatible with other introverted signs associated with water and earth: Cancer, Scorpio, Taurus, Capricorn.

• Faces possible conflict with signs sharing the same quality – mutable signs and/or those associated with fire: Gemini, Virgo, Sagittarius, Aries, Leo.

• May form a surprisingly useful pairing with the remaining signs associated with air: Libra, Aquarius.

PISCES PARTNERSHIPS

PISCES WITH	COMMENT
Aries	Insensitive – mutual understanding and rapport will be lacking.
Taurus	Intuitive – the signs will unite to hone their perception and intuition.
Gemini	Indecisive – mutual agreement and drive will be lacking.
Cancer	Flexible – both will be willing to go out of their way for the other.
Leo	One-way – Leo will intimidate and Pisces will cower.
Virgo	Uncomfortable – Pisces' wavering emotions will cause stable Virgo discomfort.
Libra	Harmonious – each will give the other a great deal of consideration.
Scorpio	Supportive – working together, both signs will find emotional harmony.
Sagittarius	Unstable – neither sign will help the other to find and appreciate stability.
Capricorn	Adaptable – Pisces will provide flexibility and Capricorn direction.
Aquarius	Complementary – Aquarius will provide Pisces with objectivity.
Pisces	Creativity – acute intuitiveness will fuel the creativity of both.

Star Signs
and Team Building

Using what we know about star sign associations and the links between the signs (see pages 10–13 and the table on page 79), we can determine the relative strengths, possible weaknesses and overall effectiveness of teams in the workplace.

Cardinal Signs
Aries, Cancer, Libra, Capricorn

Cardinal star signs (see page 11) have a natural talent for searching out new and exciting business endeavors. They are the enterprising self-starters of the zodiac who demonstrate considerable initiative and drive. In a team environment their ideal role is creating or endorsing new ideas and seeking out the required human and capital resources.

Teams with a Predominance of Cardinal Signs

This is a highly self-motivated combination. However, the initial burst of energy and focus cannot be maintained, making it difficult for teams of this type to muster the persistence needed for seeing their projects through to completion.

Teams with mostly cardinal signs may also be marred by impatience and intolerance of slower paced individuals and/or bureaucratic processes and procedures. This may lead in turn to ruthless behavior.

Teams with Few or No Cardinal Signs

These teams lack the necessary upfront initiative and motivation. During the project design or implementation phase, opportunities are soon missed or failure experienced. The teams may be disbanded quickly due to their lack of observable results. Alternatively, they may call in additional resources, such as external consultants, to help them through the early stages of new projects.

STAR SIGN, POLARITY, ELEMENT	UNIQUE TALENT	IDEAL TEAM ROLE
Aries Positive Fire	Can generate momentum and action by sheer force of will.	Change agent Leader
Libra Positive Air	Can create and establish effective relationships within and outside the team.	Networker Arbitrator
Cancer Negative Water	Can foster an emotionally secure and cohesive environment.	Team builder Nurturer
Capricorn Negative Earth	Can establish solid financial and capital foundations.	Architect Problem solver

Fixed Signs
Taurus, Leo, Scorpio, Aquarius

Fixed star signs (see page 11) have a natural talent for transforming a raw design into a finished product. Their sense of achievement comes from seeing the end results of new ideas or innovations. They thrive on challenge and pressure, demonstrating endurance, persistence, focus and stability. In a team environment their role is to maintain a result-focused approach and produce the desired outcomes.

Teams with a Majority of Fixed Signs

This combination demonstrates significant "muscle," perseverance and focus. Unfortunately, however, this mix may turn into stubborn resistance and an inability to change. Teams like these will be hampered by their overreliance on the old, familiar ways of doing things.

Teams with Few or No Fixed Signs

Teams like these do not appear to have any backbone. They lack the strong core that would enable them to press ahead and overcome obstacles and criticism. They are either all talk and no action, or too much action with few results. They soon lose the respect of others within the organization.

STAR SIGN, POLARITY, ELEMENT	UNIQUE TALENT	IDEAL TEAM ROLE
Leo Positive Fire	Can assume control effortlessly, providing consistent direction and encouragement till the end.	Leader Spokesperson
Aquarius Positive Air	Can maintain belief in own unique ideas and ideals, in the process winning others over to own point of view.	Idealist "Keeper of the faith"
Scorpio Negative Water	Can maintain emotional stability. Can remain calm and detached in a crisis.	Troubleshooter Problem solver
Taurus Negative Earth	Can provide essential physical and mental support and stability.	Loyal supporter Quiet achiever

Mutable Signs
Gemini, Virgo, Sagittarius, Pisces

Mutable star signs (see page 11) have a natural talent for uniting the cardinal and fixed signs. They are the essential jack-of-all-trades. They are resourceful, adaptable, flexible and genuinely easygoing people, and somehow bring things together without much fuss or coercion. Unlike the cardinal signs, who seek out change, or the fixed signs, who resist change, mutable signs readily embrace change.

Teams with a Predominance of Mutable Signs

This combination lacks stability and direction. While teams of this type appear positive and productive, they do in fact waste much time on dead-end discussions and mundane activities. Without strong leadership, these teams' talents are underutilized and their energies soon dissipate, leaving individual members with a feeling of restlessness.

Teams with Few or No Mutable Signs

In teams of this kind, a clash of egos may erupt, causing a lack of cooperation. Such teams may strike others as too rigid and/or overwhelming. Their inflexible, tunnel-vision approach may translate into an inability to adapt to change. A team lacking mutable signs may soon lose perspective, and its fate may be either to implode, or to face isolation from the rest of the organization.

STAR SIGN, POLARITY, ELEMENT	UNIQUE TALENT	IDEAL TEAM ROLE
Sagittarius Positive Fire	Can provide enthusiasm, light-heartedness and a willingness to be the guinea pig if necessary.	Volunteer Eager team player
Gemini Positive Air	Can support new ideas and innovative approaches. Able to translate these into tangible opportunities.	Communicator Presenter
Pisces Negative Water	Willingness to work effectively in any culture.	Jack-of-all-trades Friendly supporter
Virgo Negative Earth	Can provide critical analysis and thoroughness with processes and procedures.	Quality assurance Competent supporter

Star Signs and Career Advancement

In the work environment, good relations with our colleagues and bosses are vital – particularly if we want to advance our careers. This section highlights the most marked characteristics of each star sign. This knowledge will help you to communicate effectively with all the varying personalities you encounter in a work situation.

Extroverted Fire Signs – Aries, Leo, Sagittarius

Extroverted fire signs are open, expressive and passionate communicators. They are quick thinking and acting. When you are communicating with this group it is essential to be upfront and dramatic, and approach them with much enthusiasm and fanfare.

Aries

Arians need to be the first at everything. They need to hear words and phrases like these: "exclusive," "never before released," "first time ever," "ground breaking."

Leo

Leos are egotists and crave others' admiration. They need to hear words and phrases like these: "great," "awesome," "one and only", "the latest and the best."

Sagittarius

Sagittarians are extremely talkative, so it's best to play the excited listener with them. Ask carefully considered and sequential questions that start with "What," "How," and "Why" or "Tell me more …," to lead them eventually down the path you want them to take.

Extroverted Air Signs – Gemini, Libra, Aquarius

Extroverted air signs are gifted and intelligent communicators. They are very knowledgeable, and enjoy sharing what they know with others. When communicating with this group it's essential to be ready for, and open to, discussion and objective debate.

Gemini

Geminis' extremely active minds mean they are quickly distracted. They need to be kept on track, so be ready with "As we were saying …," "Going back to the matter at hand …," and so on.

Libra

Librans' goal is to find the status quo. They live happily with the "gray areas" on most matters. They need to hear "common ground," "unanimous approval," "politically correct."

Aquarius

Aquarians can be so eccentric it may be difficult to follow their train of thought. Paper and pen must be available at all times to capture the details of their ideas and innovations. Check for mutual understanding before moving on to the next item.

Introverted Earth Signs

Introverted earth signs prefer to knuckle down and get on with things rather than wasting time with "chit chat." When communicating with this group it is essential to gain their full attention, state the purpose upfront, and then be concise and direct.

Taurus

Taureans are happiest when they can blend work with their love of food, wine and aesthetically pleasing surroundings. Invite Taureans out for a short working lunch, coffee or drink and then, once you are settled, open a one-on-one discussion.

Virgo

Virgoans are perfectionists who worry a lot and need reassuring regularly. Approach a Virgoan as the "expert" – the "only one" who can "competently" attend to the task.

Capricorn

Capricorns find complexity and problem solving terribly attractive. Approach them armed with facts, figures and copious information. Present the issue as a "problem" too complex for you to solve – and then watch them go.

Introverted Water Signs

Introverted water signs are ruled by their hearts, and have a largely subjective approach. When communicating with this group it is essential to demonstrate empathy, take time to build rapport and ask them how they "feel" about things.

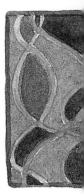

Cancer

Cancerians are addicted to nurturing others while hiding themselves. Don't approach them directly – they will put up a wall. Rather, pose hypothetical questions. Share your feelings and ask them for guidance.

Scorpio

Scorpios keep their cards close to their chests. They like to be communicated with "in confidence." Approach them with "secret" or "sensitive" information to gain their attention.

Pisces

Pisceans need time to absorb information and clarify their feelings and thoughts before responding. Give them pre-reading material before meetings, and don't expect definite answers immediately.

Star Signs and Stress Management

The following table suggests ways for each star sign to deal appropriately with stress at work, and to maintain general good health.

STAR SIGN HEALTH NOTES	TELLTALE SIGNS OF STRESS	TECHNIQUES TO MANAGE STRESS
Aries A strong constitution, a quick healer	Accidents, injuries, migraines, headaches, fever (fire nature)	Regular and vigorous exercise, active sports, healthy diet
Taurus Tends to avoid exercise, more a spectator than a participant in sports, resilient constitution, represses feelings	Weight increase, depression, bad temper, sore throat, laryngitis, swollen glands, stiff neck, constipation	Physical activity – walking, cycling, massage, regular stretches, yoga
Gemini A lot of natural vitality, active metabolism, tends to neglect health, prone to burnout/ chronic stress, a reluctant patient, quick to recover	Mental exhaustion, coughs, colds, flu	Group/team sports, tennis/squash, meditation, tai chi, yoga, time out each day to rest mind and body, sleep

STAR SIGN HEALTH NOTES	TELLTALE SIGNS OF STRESS	TECHNIQUES TO MANAGE STRESS
Cancer Tends to suffer in silence, when depressed is susceptible to everything going around	Anxiety, infectious diseases, indigestion, eating disorders such as anorexia and bulimia	Maintaining healthy personal and work relationships, counselling, relaxation, water sports, solitude – taking long walks, etc., to recharge
Leo A naturally strong constitution, takes health for granted, gets run down easily	Injuries/accidents, high blood pressure, hypertension, back pain, "bad back"	Rest/relaxation, low-fat diet, cardiovascular exercise, dancing, strengthening and stretching exercises for lower back muscles
Virgo Disciplined – tends to look after self, an active interest in health and the body; worry is the greatest health threat	Hypochondria, irritable bowel syndrome, eczema	Getting back to nature – solitary walks, meditation, relaxation, facials/massages

STAR SIGN HEALTH NOTES	TELLTALE SIGNS OF STRESS	TECHNIQUES TO MANAGE STRESS
Libra Lazy about exercise, desire to look after self motivated by vanity, can quickly become stressed when one area of life dominates others	Chronic tiredness, sluggish metabolism	Dancing, light exercise, health clubs, Eastern remedies, avoiding isolation – maintaining active social life
Scorpio Plenty of natural stamina, takes health for granted, pushes self to limits, suffers from a build-up of toxins in body	Psychosomatic illnesses, bladder infections, thrush	Physically demanding activity, water sports, massage, total relaxation, short cleansing diets
Sagittarius Naturally active/physical lifestyle, rarely ill – quick to recover, maintains a cheerful optimism when in pain, fondness for rich foods and wines: indulgent streak can tax liver	Accidents/injuries, arthritis, rheumatism, pain in hips and legs	Avoid damp and confined areas, maintain regular activity, ease off on the passion for adventure sports, diet when necessary

STAR SIGN HEALTH NOTES	TELLTALE SIGNS OF STRESS	TECHNIQUES TO MANAGE STRESS
Capricorn Naturally hard working, a strong constitution, an aversion to exercise – prefers desk-bound lifestyle	Worry, moodiness, dental problems, general pessimism, chronic illnesses – depression/ skin problems	General cheering up – a visit to the local comedy club; learning to laugh at problems, developing a more optimistic outlook, practicing moderation in everything, yoga/ stretching, light aerobic exercise
Aquarius Not naturally in tune with body's needs, physically inactive, difficulty adjusting to hot/ cold weather	Numbness in hands/feet, sprains, circulatory problems, varicose veins, sudden illnesses	Getting out into the fresh air, aerobic exercise, pedicures, massages
Pisces Health directly affected by feelings and moods, prone to addictions	Illnesses mostly of psychosomatic origin, excessive drinking/use of drugs, warts, corns, bunions, swelling, chilblains	Massage, avoiding stimulants, psychiatry/ counseling, good shoes

Finding Out More

Birth Charts

Your star sign is determined by the position of the Sun in the heavens at the time of your birth. The Sun is the core, life-giving force of our solar system. However, this is only part of the total picture, as the position of the Moon and the planets also influences the personality. Birth charts give an indication of the positions of all the planets at the moment of birth, and the significance of this. For example, the Moon may have been in Libra at the time of your birth and this means you may share some of the Libran's emotional characteristics. Having your birth chart prepared and interpreted by a professional is recommended if your interest in astrology extends past the focus of this book.

Reading List

Goldschneider, Gary, *The Secret Language of Birthdays – Personology Profiles for Each Day of the Year*, Penguin Studio, 1994. (ISBN 0670858579)

Goldschneider, Gary, and Elffers, Joost, *The Secret Language of Relationships – Your Complete Personology Guide to Any Relationship*, Penguin Studio, 1997. (ISBN 0670875279)

Goodman, Linda, *Linda Goodman's Sun Signs*, Taplinger Publishing Company, 1968. (ISBN 0800849000)

Greene, Liz and Sasportas, Howard, *The Luminaries: The Psychology of the Sun and Moon in the Horoscopes*, Red Wheel/Weiser, 1992. (ISBN 0877287503)

Guttman, Ariel, Johnson, Kenneth and Guttman, Gail, *Mythic Astrology: Archetypal Powers in the Horoscope*, Llewellyn Publications, 1993. (ISBN 0875422489)

Hickey, Isabel M., *Astrology, A Cosmic Science*, CRCS Publications, 1992. (ISBN 0916360520)

Renstrom, Christopher, *Ruling Planets: Your Astrological Guide to Life's Ups and Downs*, HarperCollins, 2002. (ISBN 006019992)

Stathis, Georgia, *Business Astrology 101: Weaving the Web Between Business and Myth*, Starcycles, 2001. (ISBN 1881229262)

STAR SIGN	RULING PLANET	POLARITY	ELEMENT	QUALITY
Aries March 21–April 19	Mars	Positive	Fire	Cardinal
Taurus April 20–May 20	Venus	Negative	Earth	Fixed
Gemini May 21–June 20	Mercury	Positive	Air	Mutable
Cancer June 21–July 22	Moon	Negative	Water	Cardinal
Leo July 23–August 22	Sun	Positive	Fire	Fixed
Virgo August 23–September 22	Mercury	Negative	Earth	Mutable
Libra September 23–October 22	Venus	Positive	Air	Cardinal
Scorpio October 23–November 21	Pluto and Mars	Negative	Water	Fixed
Sagittarius November 22–December 21	Jupiter	Positive	Fire	Mutable
Capricorn December 22–January 19	Saturn	Negative	Earth	Cardinal
Aquarius January 20–February 18	Uranus and Saturn	Positive	Air	Fixed
Pisces February 19–March 20	Neptune and Jupiter	Negative	Water	Mutable

Published in 2003 by Lansdowne Publishing Pty Ltd
Level 1, 18 Argyle Street, Sydney NSW 2000, Australia

First published in the United States in 2003 by
Red Wheel/Weiser LLC
York Beach, ME
With offices at:
368 Congress Street
Boston, MA 02210
www.redwheelweiser.com

Commissioned by Deborah Nixon
Text: Debbie Burns
Illustrations: Penny Lovelock and Sue Ninham
Design: Sue Rawkins
Copy Editor: Avril Janks
Production Manager: Sally Stokes
Project Coordinator: Kate Merrifield

ISBN 1-59003-068-0

Set in Goudy, Humanist, and Orange on QuarkXPress
Printed in Singapore by Tien Wah Press (Pte) Ltd